The Greatness Game

The Greatness Game

Inspired ways to live, love, and lead like you mean it.

By

DENA PATTON

www.DenaPatton.com

The Greatness Game

To contact the author or request bulk quantities of The Greatness Game, please email admin@DenaPatton.com.

ISBN: 978-0-9988544-0-3

Illustrations by Alexandra Patton

Cover and layout designed by Niche Pressworks

Edited by Shay Moser

To my husband, who has been my rock. Thank you for loving me and helping me step into my greatness. To our daughter, Alli, who is the light of our life, and who is my biggest greatness teacher. Thank you for choosing me as your mom. To my mom, my heaven angel who always believed in the goodness and greatness of life. To God, for being patient and never giving up on my greatness.

Special thanks to Nicole Gebhardt from Niche Pressworks, Diana Rinkoff, Shay Moser, and Diane Markins for your support.

"A bird sitting on a tree is never afraid of the branch breaking, because her **trust** is not on the branch but on her **own wings.**"

Introduction

This book might be small — and that is by design. It is a powerful, daily manual to keep with you to maintain your greatness. I teach this methodology through speaking, coaching and writing because I want people to win the games that are most important to them. This methodology is a revolutionary way to help you identify the invisible smallness agreements that can limit and constrain your greatness. What would be possible if you could access 100 percent of your greatest self?

I wrote this in the same way I would give tips to you in a conversation over coffee. As I often say, "Communication *without action* is just another conversation," so I encourage you to take action. There will be some tips that you are already living, but I want you to look for the ones that can change everything for you. Nothing changes if nothing changes; therefore "The Greatness Game" is about taking action and changing the game. The tips in this book will teach you to crush smallness so that you can live, love and lead from your greatness and create the most extraordinary life you can imagine. Play to win!

Cheers to your greatness,

Dena

Table of Contents

The Greatness Game...1

The Greatness Leadership..............................17

The Greatness Marriage 31

The Greatness Entrepreneur............................. 43

The Greatness Faith.. 65

The Greatness Life.. 83

The Greatness Money...................................... 103

The Greatness Parenting 111

The Greatness Girls 121

The Greatness Game

I'm a girl from a dysfunctional family who was raised by a single mom, yet somehow I believed I was made for more. I had NO evidence of that, but I also didn't want to become a statistic. I wanted to overcome my past and the nasty smallness voice that told me, "You are from the wrong family to dream big" and "You are too stupid." I allowed smallness to rob 27 years of my life. I didn't know any better. I didn't let that define me. Instead, it refined me.

It took a minor stroke at 27 for me to ignite my greatness. I had to overcome the grips of smallness by unbelieving and unlearning the smallness statements that I subconsciously agreed to over the years. I chose to come OUT of agreement with every single one of them. Those beliefs were dragging my life, my gifts, my dreams and my income down. What we believe is what we become, and when I started to listen to my greatness voice instead of my smallness voice, my life changed forever. Then in 2005, I started coaching others to do the same.

The power to believe and agree with your greatness voice is already within you. It is a choice to come out of agreement with your smallness. Imagine your life is a train, and greatness wants you to *stay on track* to achieve your big dreams and greatest potential. Smallness intends to *derail the train*, so you never get there. Smallness feeds you negative and disempowering statements, such as "I'm not enough," "I can't do this," I'm the wrong color," "I'm too (fill in the blank)" to deflate and derail you. It's like an abusive friend who wants to control you.

I want you to tell your smallness that the game is over. You are now empowered with 115 tips that will help you win the greatness game. I encourage you *to play to win*, don't just play to play. You have amazing dreams and greatness to share with the world. You are unlimited when you live, love and lead from your greatness. I filled this book with tips, resources, free downloads and lots of love to help you win your greatness games. I hope you enjoy it.

Smallness loves blaming and shaming others. Let's just say that responsibility and accountability are not games of smallness. When you truly want to achieve your greatest dreams and your greatness potential, then taking responsibility and accountability for your beliefs, actions and results are key.

Having moments where you fail or trip are part of practicing a new skill. As you start to live, love and lead from your greatness, it starts with one choice then it will take practice to master. Give yourself grace and space to learn this new skill. You will get better over time, and you will master your greatness mindset. Play to win, don't play to play.

Why is smallness powerful? How can it sabotage and derail us successfully? That's because it's good at making you distrust yourself, and distrust is the beginning of self-destruction and self-sabotage. Often, it gets in the way of your life, relationships and dreams, but if you are experiencing things like self-harm, cutting or suicidal thoughts, I encourage you to reach out to mentalhealth.gov for free resources. Your mental health is important, and you matter.

What do you think this world would be like if every person on the planet never heard their smallness voice again? It starts with you, then watch the ripple effect. Take on the Greatness Game for 90 days and watch how your joy, peace, gratitude, fulfillment and happiness grow.

It's a beautiful thing when you allow yourself to be in the duality of being an expert AND being a student. You are an expert in many things, but when you keep an open mind always to be learning, you become a better expert.

There is a great saying that I love: "Plan your work and work your plan." Sometimes we forget to plan, or we start projects that we never finish. When you plan your dreams, and weekly and annual projects, it helps you stay on track with the vision YOU want for your life. When we don't plan, we often get tangled in smallness and get derailed. Take a look at all the things that you have that are unfinished, and get rid of the ones that don't matter, and only keep the ones that you will plan out and finish.

Who comes to mind when you think of role models that you admire and who live with authenticity and greatness? How can you use their story to inspire you? What is one thing they did that you can do that could change everything? The people who influenced me heavily were my mom and dad, my Greek grandmother, Mayor Rudy Giuliani (In 1996, I was living in NYC, and he was the first politician that I saw fulfill his promises without making excuses, and he was fantastic during 9/11.), Ellen DeGeneres and Oprah Winfrey.

Get rid of anything that ties you to your smallness. We tend to clutter our lives with more stuff, especially with stuff that can keep us tied to smallness or trigger smallness. It might be in your car, your wardrobe, your desk, your purse/bag, your house, your food or in your office. Do a "smallness inventory" in all those places, and throw out anything that doesn't serve your greatness and your dreams.

Smallness loves having pity parties. But when you live from your greatness, pity parties are too short even to have enough time to invite anyone to them.

Let's talk about drama. We have a choice to create drama, attract drama or engage in drama. It's a smallness game to keep us in chaos, overwhelm, distraction and far away from our greatness and dreams. The best thing to do is break up with it. Start a new policy to stop creating, attracting or engaging in drama, and you will see that you gain more peace, joy and clarity.

A quick overview

INTUITION: It's an internal 'warning system' that gives you red-flags to help you "course correct" when you are going down the wrong road.

FEELINGS: The beautiful experience of being human. Learn to honor and have your feelings verses letting your feelings control you.

GREATNESS VOICE: The "little voice" in your head that empowers you to become your greatest potential and fulfill your greatest dreams (turn it up!).

SMALLNESS VOICE: The "other little voice" that disempowers you with smallness games, and doesn't want you to win so it can control you (turn it down!).

The Greatness Leadership

The greatness game is a process to master your greatness mindset and unleash your greatest potential so you can live, love and lead like you mean it. Whether you are leading a family, team, class, company, community or movement, it will be drastically different if you are leading from your greatness rather than leading from your smallness. It took a minor stroke at age 27, which was my blessed interruption, for me to meet my greatness, and I've been leading from it ever since. These are a few of my favorite tips to win your Greatness Game in Leadership.

In leadership, values often dictate how people show up, speak, act and treat others. Knowing your core values and making them a fundamental part of your leadership, parenting and life are a greatness game that is worth winning. One of my favorite tips for business owners is to hire, fire and lead by your values. In business, the fastest way to get derailed and off track is to compromise your values. Check the back of this book for a reading recommendation on this subject.

Leadership is not about perfection; it's about your greatness, so let's change the game. Your greatness sparks others' greatness, your excellence sparks others' excellence, but sometimes smallness takes over. The five big games of smallness are: P.D.F.O.D. = Perfection, Distraction, Fear, Overwhelm and Doubt. Are you tangled up in any of these smallness games? When you are playing smallness games, you lose what's important. Come out of agreement with that smallness belief (i.e. I have to be perfect), and you'll change the game.

Your thoughts become your words. Your words become your actions. Your actions become your habits. And your habits become your results. What you think and what you believe will then affect everything after that. It's a domino effect because it's all connected. The thing to master is self-discipline so that you think only from your greatness. It takes practice, just like a basketball game, but with practice, you get great at it. In every moment, you have the choice to believe your smallness or believe your greatness. Choose wisely.

When you have a tough decision to make between two things, for example, a work conference or your child's dance recital, try using the 10-10-10 idea by Suzy Welch. Ask yourself if it will affect your daughter in 10 minutes, 10 months or 10 years from now. As a leader, you often face hard choices, but this is a quick way to determine if the impact will be a short cry or something that will follow you (or the other person) forever.

Do you often feel overwhelmed or distracted? Those are two big games of smallness that can derail your train. One of the greatest temptations is to give into smallness games, but now you know better. Keep on track by working in *priority order*. I encourage you to review your priorities on a daily or weekly basis, then manage your time accordingly. It will take boundaries and focus not to allow your plate to overflow. Remember, "no" is a complete sentence. I created an easy priority list template with directions that you can download free at www.amazinggreatness.com.

Leadership is an action, not a title. Whether you are a top CEO or on a PTA, it is who *you are being* in your daily actions that you will be known for. Think of two words that you would love to be known for and start *being* those words in all of your actions and leadership. That is a game worth winning.

Three of the biggest assets that you have to use in life are your voice, your power and your money. I call them your Trifecta of Greatness. How do you currently use your Trifecta? How do you dream of using your Trifecta? Can you think of people who used their voice, power or money to change the world in big or small ways? It's hard to be powerful with your Trifecta when smallness has a grip on your mindset. So I want you to remember that you are powerful, and with practice you can master your greatness mindset and do great things with your Trifecta.

Courage is extremely underestimated. I have found that *courage* is at the heart of all of my success, and *fear* is at the heart of all of my failures. Courage is vital to winning greatness games. When you have big greatness games and big dreams to pursue, you will need a hefty load of courage for the good times and for the hard times. On a scale of 1 to 10, where would you rate your courage? If you want to raise your courage score, then do things that scare you — A LOT.

I remember the first time someone said to me, "How you do one thing is how you do everything." Don't get offended before you let it soak in. Whether you play at 50 percent or 85 percent, I challenge you to play at 100 percent this week. Look at how you "do" your checkbook/budget, your marriage/relationships, your reports, your self-care, your laundry, or even how you return the shopping cart in the parking lot. To win greatness games, I encourage you to play at 100 percent. Start today.

You want to be very aware of who or what might be stealing your greatness. This week I want you to track every time you get disempowered or triggered in smallness. It's not fun to confront your smallness triggers (P.D.F.O.D. = **P**erfection, **D**istraction, **F**ear, **O**verwhelm and **D**oubt), but it is a part of this process. The more you know about your triggers the more you can *prevent* them, *avoid* them or *transform* them. I did this exercise over an entire year so that I could officially #crushsmallness and master my greatness mindset.

Next time you feel yourself forcing something to happen, ask yourself why you're forcing it to happen, and be willing to listen and course correct if you can. When we force things to happen, we are often coming from fear, which is a game of smallness. But when we are in our flow, we are in a game of greatness. Trusting your "flow" is allowing yourself, your gifts and your greatness to flow powerfully and naturally.

A quick overview

Want to really change the game from smallness to greatness? Take the #crushsmallness 30 Day Challenge where you and a buddy work on crushing your smallness every time you hear it. This will help you build your greatness 'muscle' and master your greatness mindset. Your life goes where your mind goes - so when you focus on training your mindset to think from #greatnessonly it will change your life. Support each other, help each other and encourage each other for 30 days to only think, act and speak from greatness.

The Greatness Marriage

Whether you are married or not, we all have relationships in our lives. The richness of life is in the quality of our relationships. I believe that marriage is such a blessing and I treat it like a precious gift. I met my husband through online dating 14 years ago, and one thing he knows how to do is love. It is his superpower. Being his wife through all the ups and downs of life hasn't made me a marriage expert. However, success leaves clues. These are my tips to win your Greatness Game in Marriage.

Don't let life drag your marriage down or pull it apart. Remember to have boundaries so that other roles, situations, work or people don't tear your marriage apart. Put your marriage as your top priority and protect it. If you don't protect it AND respect it, then don't expect others to do the same.

Have fun! Laughing and enjoying each other is crucial to a successful marriage — whether it's a date night at the comedy club or enjoying a stroll in the park. Fun can easily get squeezed out of life, so you must be intentional about keeping it alive. Every New Year's Day, we create a Play List with our top 10 things that we want to do for fun that year. In 2015, Paris was on the list, and we made it happen! You can download the Play List template for free at www.amazinggreatness.com.

The six greatness pillars of a successful marriage are respect, communication, love, integrity, fun and God. The fastest way to gage these pillars for your relationship is to rate each one of them from a 1 to 10. You want to shoot for an 8 or higher. However, the beauty is that you can improve any score below eight by getting in action. Read a book on that subject. Take a workshop. Hire a counselor or a relationship coach.

> "Once you know better you can do better."
> — MAYA ANGELOU

Love him or her in *their* love language. According to author Gary Chapman, there are five love languages. Your love language is the "language" in which you express your love, AND how you prefer to be loved. The five languages are physical touch, quality time, gift giving, acts of service or words of affirmation. When we love someone (our kids, our employees, our spouse) in *his or her* love language, it changes the game.

> * See the book list in the back about love languages.

Are you struggling in your relationship? Make a list of ALL the ways you would improve your next relationship if you weren't in your current relationship. Now, take that list and do them for your significant other. Sometimes we just have to break the current patterns and start doing things differently. See the book list in the back about a great book on this subject.

Marriage is a game worth winning. Don't just play to play. Play 100 percent like you mean it. Promise yourself today that you will quit any nagging, jabbing, poking, criticizing, demeaning, dismissing or disempowering your spouse. When you see yourself doing smallness behaviors, I encourage you to have the greatness and courage to break the cycle. What you allow continues, and that pertains to your behavior and how others treat you.

Forgive often because unforgiveness grows resentment and anger. If you have unexplained bitterness or hostility when your significant other walks in the room, that might be a sign of unforgiveness. The key is forgiveness. Start by forgiving him for loading the dishwasher wrong or forgiving her for spending money on shoes. I have been there, and I didn't even know how I got there. It *takes time* to truly see all the little things and all the big things that might be eating at your heart, but it is worth it. You will get your joy, connection and love back!

Chill out. When we are managing a home, bills, kids, schedules, jobs and marriage, we can get tight and crunchy. That's when smallness can come in and spin you out of control. Try starting a morning (or evening) routine where you can chill out for 10 minutes for prayer/ meditation/journal time to do three things: 1) Ground yourself in your greatness and see if any smallness is "at play." 2) Check for any red flags to which you need to listen. 3) Be in gratitude for all your blessings (current ones and future ones that are on their way).

To love and be loved.

That is the purpose of life.

The rest is just a distraction.

The Greatness Entrepreneur

I've been an entrepreneur for 20 years and sold my public relations and marketing company in NYC in 1999. From that experience, I've come to believe that our careers aren't about to-do lists and accomplishments. Instead, they are the best delivery platform for our greatness. Think about wildly successful people like Oprah, Michael Jordan, Ellen DeGeneres and Katy Perry. They have mastered not only their greatness mindset, but they use their platforms to share their greatness and gifts unapologetically. These are my tips to win your Greatness Game in Entrepreneurship (you can apply most to life or any career).

There are many ups and downs in business, but a fun way to track the daily or weekly successes is to start a winning wall. It could be a white board, a chalk walk or get creative with sticky vinyl. When you have a win or "move the train", write it on the winning wall. You will be shocked at how motivating it is to watch the successes grow over the month. If you have employees, get them in on it, too, and have a community winning wall. Reading everyone's wins is great! #winningwall

As an entrepreneur coach, one of the first exercises I have clients complete is clarifying three essential things that change your business game. *Your vision, your purpose and your values.* Pull out a piece of paper and draw a straight, vertical train track, then draw a train (represents your business). At the end of the track is your three-year vision that pulls the train toward it, on both sides of the track are your values that keep you ON track, and behind the train is your purpose/your "why" that motivates and pushes the train toward the big vision.

Kevin Hall said, "When you know your why, you know your way," which is one of my favorite principles of life. For every speech, project, book or business I have created, it's the "why" that keeps the train moving forward with clarity and momentum. Smallness mindsets just force the train down the track and often get derailed. Greatness mindsets know *why they are moving the train* and win at their big vision.

Don't just create a company, build a *great* company. Win this greatness game by leading your business from your greatness every day. When you make mistakes, forgive yourself (quickly), and don't let smallness convince you that you are not able, not enough, not right or not a good leader. Get re-centered and start moving the train again. There will be smallness opportunities to get derailed, especially when you are playing big, that's why it's important to have grace with yourself.

It's who you are being (thoughts/beliefs) that dictates your doing (actions), which dictates your having (results). If you want a particular result, then always start with figuring out who you need to be? Do you need to be focused, loving, powerful or courageous? Who do you have to BE to accomplish your top priorities today? Who do you have to BE to achieve your one big dream this year? Who do you have to BE to perform your top greatness game?

If your dream is to build a million-dollar business, there are many systems, structures, strategies and schedules you have to have in place. My former client Russ Perry, CEO of www.designpickle.com, is an example that the fastest way to go from an idea to owning a million-dollar-plus business is to show up in your greatness and BE a million-dollar CEO from day one. It's very different than being a $100,000 CEO. You think, act, lead, delegate and market differently. BE a million-dollar CEO. #milliondollarceochallenge

Laser focus moves the train. It's super fun to look at shiny objects, but remember distraction is a smallness game. It will get you way off track and cost you a lot of money and time. If you really want to move the train toward your big vision, then laser focus will be your best friend.

If you are struggling and feel overwhelmed in smallness, I want you to remember not to use your energy to quit, use it *to finish*. Change the game from struggling to finishing. Take it one day at a time and keep turning down the smallness voice that gets you tangled up. Focus on making small wins and hold on to God, *not* your pain. Make God your CEO and watch your business thrive. You. Can. Do. This.

It was in the middle of a coaching call when one of my dear clients paused in a long silence and then said, "My whole life I have been playing big games, and winning. I win most of the things I play. BUT, I've been playing the wrong games until now." I responded, "That will go in my book someday!" This example is a reminder that you are always winning the games you are playing. Make them greatness games.

Communication *without action* is just another conversation. Action is the key to moving the train.

Whether you sell products or services, you have to be different. Don't be afraid of adding your unique greatness and gifts so that you're not like everyone else in your industry. It's your uniqueness that makes people buy from you *so don't hide it*. For instance, there are a ton of coaches and most of them host masterminds, but because I love fun and adventure, I host one-day Skydiving Masterminds called Jump Into Greatness for leaders and entrepreneurs. They sell out because they are different and a great expression of my greatness. Think differently.

You can't win the entrepreneur game without talking about your customers. Here are four important questions about your target market: 1) When it comes to your target market, do you know who your *ideal* clients are and where to find them? 2) Do *they* know they need you (if not, your marketing completely shifts)? 3) Are you consistently marketing and getting in front of them online and offline? 4) Do your ideal clients rave about you and refer you. If not, why?

Have you ever felt like you are burning yourself out? A paramount thing to have in any career are boundaries to prevent you from imploding. Your health, your marriage and your life are worth more than a job. However, smallness will argue with you on this matter. Don't believe the temptation that there is no difference between "working late" and working yourself to death. Self-care is one of the most important pillars of greatness. If you want to win in this area, download my free Self-Care Plan template at www.amazinggreatness.com.

Your title is not who you are. The same goes for your degree. They are great accomplishments, but you are much more than the sum of your successes. Your self-esteem doesn't depend on titles, money, awards or roles. It's a choice to believe in yourself despite all of your triumphs. Can you believe in yourself just as you are and just as you aren't? Self-esteem determines our self-worth, which determines how much we earn/charge, so it's a good choice to believe in yourself and your greatness. This is not about ego. It's about owning and sharing your greatness.

Your gifts and greatness were gifts from God, and your gift back to Him is owning, using and sharing them with the world through your platforms and roles.

The day you realize that you aren't meant to serve everyone, you realize whom you *truly* are here to serve. Not everyone is your customer, and that is ok. #NOTMYTRIBE

Go-getters are good, but go-getters who are also go-givers are even better. Consider creating a ministry or a philanthropy element in your business. Don't make it complicated or hard, just a simple way to give back. It is good for the company, you, employee engagement and benefactors. Spreading goodness and greatness never did a company wrong.

Dear past, thank you for all the lessons. Dear future, I am ready.

There are eight areas of business, all of which are important and build on one another. Whether you are in your first or 20th year of being a business owner, it is wise to do a "tuneup" each year to check all the systems, numbers, processes and progress of the eight areas. You can see the list of these eight areas at www.8areasofbusiness.com.

The Greatness Faith

I wrote this section to help ignite your faith, whatever religion or spiritual stage you are in, so that your faith is **alive** in **all** areas of your life. When we can free our faith from being in a compartmentalized box labeled "my faith," we can start living authentically and powerfully. I started my Christian walk at age 14 and it has been my saving grace and the reason I have the life, marriage and business that I have. God is good and these are a few of my tips to win your Greatness Game in Faith.

What you focus on expands. Focusing on your faith will provide you with a deeper understanding of yourself, your God, your life, your death, your purpose and everything in between. You can go deeper by reading books, getting involved in small groups or Bible studies, or attending a retreat or conference.

If you are going to play big games in business or life, then your spiritual game has to be equally significant. Don't make the mistake of getting to a certain level of success and then leave your religious practices in the dust. You need faith to get to the top, but you also need it to stay on top.

Your spiritual self is the foundation of life, and if it's shattered, everything else becomes unstable. Smallness will try to make you believe that your faith is not needed, but I assure you that it is crucial to winning greatness games. It not only improves your spiritual game but it "raises all the boats" by improving your marriage, your perspective, your job and your life.

Is God calling you to a particular spiritual calling, and you don't feel ready or equipped? It will be a lot easier if you get smallness (fear and doubt) out of the picture. Trust that you don't need to have all the answers, nor do you need to see God's "entire plan." Just say yes and trust God has it all figured out.

"A bird sitting on a tree is never afraid of the branch breaking, because her **trust** is not on the branch but on her own **wings**. Always believe in yourself"

- UNKNOWN

Consider that your wings, your greatness, your gifts and your God can be trusted 100 percent.

You have an opportunity to work with God every day
by sharing your gifts and greatness out into the world.
Beware that smallness will try to derail you by feeding you
one of it's Big Five Games (P.D.F.O.D – Perfectionism,
Doubt, Fear, Overwhelm, Distraction). Don't fall for it.
It's up to you if you are going to listen to your smallness
voice or your greatness voice. #crushsmallness

Reaching a new level means there could be a new "devil." You are playing big games in your life, and with every new level that you accomplish, there may be a challenge, a trial, a barrier or a smallness attack. Be prepared. The faster you can overcome it, the faster you will get back on track. Don't let that little smallness "devil" derail you again.

Don't believe one more smallness statement that keeps you small or scared. God made you a warrior, to thrive and to overcome the temptations of smallness. You have the power and the freedom *to come out of agreement with any smallness statement.*

> For I know the plans I have for you, plans to prosper you and not to harm you, plans to give you hope and a future.
> - JEREMIAH 29:11 (NIV)

Every day, you have to choose to live, love and lead from your greatness *or* your smallness. Which one will help you achieve your greatest dreams, your spiritual calling and help you become your most awesome self?

Have you ever had a 3-year-old child manipulate or play you? Smallness is just like that. Sometimes it can be "beautiful or cute or successful enough" that it can look like greatness. But at a closer look, you see that it is smallness playing you. The entire function of smallness is to keep you in its grip so it can control you. It wants you to be far away from the things that empower you, like your dreams, gifts, greatness and God. Don't let it rob you of one more day.

If you experience a smallness attack and feel like you're quickly getting deflated and disempowered, then have a smallness release prayer ready. You can keep it on your phone in the Evernote app or somewhere handy. Use it whenever you get a smallness attack to help you get re-centered in your greatness. It's part affirmation, part prayer, part kick-your-butt back into greatness. You can write it yourself, or you can use mine (on my blog at www.DenaPatton.com in the category Leaving Smallness).

Do you think a lioness in the wild ever wakes up and doubts she is strong enough to hunt that day? No, she walks in her beautiful power and strength with *no* doubt. That is the topic in one of my favorite books *Lioness Arising,* a must read if you want renewal in your spiritual power and strength. You are that beautiful lioness ready to make a difference in the world.

When you dream from your "head," you can get tangled in logistics and smallness. But when you dream from your soul, you become unlimited. Are you ready to dream big? #dreambigger

Listening, living, loving and leading from your smallness is one of the biggest temptations you have. Every time you get deflated or disempowered by smallness, you have to save yourself, again and again. But once you start living from your greatness, you stop the vicious cycle of saving yourself, and instead, you start *standing for yourself*. It's an entirely different game.

Stop. Pray. Listen. Sometimes in our prayers, all we do is talk, ask and plead. But the real gold is in listening. Not while driving, cooking or working, but true listening without multitasking. Stop, pray and listen because it will change the game when you give God access to you.

Be careful not to get tangled up in worldly games and forget about your Godly games. Worldly games look alluring, compelling and satisfying, but usually, they distract you from what is important. How are you honoring God or glorifying Him through your roles or platforms?

The Greatness Life

Living, loving and leading from your greatness is not often taught in school or talked about openly. When I first learned about self-development in 1999, I was shocked to learn you can transform negative thoughts or limiting beliefs that hold you back. It was like a pot of gold! I fell in love with the work and trained as a coach to help people get unstuck from labels, limitations and smallness. I change people's lives, and God transforms people's hearts. These are a few of my favorite tips to win your Greatness Game in Life.

We all have past jobs and experiences that we have "left in the past." But there's probably some real "gold" that you forgot about at the old job. It might be a skill set or experience that smallness has hidden. It might be the very thing to take you to the next level. For the first five years as a business coach, I didn't mention that I had owned a PR and marketing company. Eventually, I realized that it was a valuable skill that needs to be in my marketing, and it changed the game for me. Own *all* of your greatness.

One way to help shift a smallness mindset to a greatness mindset is gratitude. When you have a daily gratitude practice, it helps you turn what you have into enough. It also helps you stop scarcity thoughts. Scarcity thinking never creates abundance, wealth, fulfillment or greatness. It's as simple as taking five minutes a day to write down what you are grateful for in life. I even made you a free 30-day Gratitude Journal that you can find at www.amazinggreatness.com.

You won't accomplish your big dreams by staying in your comfort zone. That's why many people struggle with their desires because they want to achieve their big dreams, but they don't want to leave their comfort zone. That's like wanting a gallon of ice cream from the freezer, but you're unwilling to get off the couch to get it. It might be uncomfortable leaving your comfort zone, but I promise you'll get over it quickly.

When you are playing big games in life, you are going to do a lot of receiving; it might be in the form of help, gifts, connections, money, opportunities, a door opened for you, or love and support. Greatness is humbled and open to receiving, but smallness often sabotages or denies it. How you receive *one thing* is how you receive *everything*. Observe the way you receive the next 10 things. It might surprise you.

One of the first places to start creating a life you love is in your mind, body and spirit. A self-care plan will not only strengthen you and keep you on track, but it also sets the example for your kids about how to treat yourself. How you treat yourself says a lot about whether you are living in smallness or living in greatness. Smallness doesn't care about self-care; it might try to distract you from this tip. Write down your daily, weekly and monthly items to help nurture your mind, body and spirit.

You train people how to treat you through the use of your boundaries. It's usually easier to create boundaries but harder to uphold them. But you can do it. One of the first steps is to honor your boundaries first; then people will follow suit. If you say you are going to leave the office at 5 p.m. and go to the gym, then uphold it. If you say you don't lend money to friends, then uphold it. If you say you don't get in unhealthy relationships, then uphold it.

Are you a busy mom with crazy amounts of details, schedules, meal planning, kids' homework, bills and work that make you feel overwhelmed? A dear client, April Perry, is an expert in "home systems" and helps overwhelmed moms win the home game! I love that! As I always say, "Where there is chaos, there is a lack of a system." There are specific methods that you can do at home to create a well-managed, well-run home. She has excellent resources at www.learndobecome.com.

One of my favorite quotes that Sandra Yancey always says is, "When your past calls, hang up, it has nothing new to say." Take the golden nuggets (experiences, skills and lessons) from your past and move on. Your dreams and future are waiting.

When you are feeling sorry for yourself, find someone to help or serve. Call a friend who is a single mom and see how you can help her. Help someone who is elderly or volunteer at a nonprofit that helps the homeless. Giving back and helping others always makes our pity party short lived.

More stuff doesn't make you happy. It just makes you broke.

The grieving process is real, and if you have lost someone you love, or have lost a pet or a job, then you are somewhere in the five steps of the grieving process. When I lost my mom to pancreatic cancer, it took me two years to grieve and find my "new normal." It took time, patience and grace. If you are going through a loss, it might be helpful to read books on grief, see a counselor, or attend a support group to help you navigate the emotions so that you become better, not bitter.

I'm sharing a tip from my friend Diane Markins: There are four types of friends everyone needs. They include a mentor who can offer wisdom, a mentee to whom you can offer your wisdom, a confidant and encourager who will stand by your side no matter what and a "lifter" who knows how to support you when you are down.

Whether you are seeking a job, a spouse, a dream or a best friend, always remember the great quote by Rumi, "What you are seeking is seeking you." Sometimes you have to be patient because it doesn't happen within your timeline.

What is your superpower? You know, that "gift" that you are excellent at that is effortless for you? It might be love, or greatness, or being a light or healing or forgiveness. When we know our superpower, we can serve where there is a lack of that gift. If forgiveness is your gift, go where there is shame. If it is love, go where there is hate. If it is greatness, go where there is smallness. If it is healing, go where there is sickness. If it is joy, go where there is despair.

Your personal power is like a hammer. You can choose to use it to destroy, or you can use it to create beautiful things. Using it to tear down, or "power over people" is often dominating and certainly is not leading from greatness. Your personal power is a gift that you were born with, and you can do great things with it. See the back of the book for a reading recommendation on this subject.

You were born with intuition, which is like your personal "red flag" machine. When you get a "red flag," do you tend to listen to it or ignore it? If you look back on the big "mistakes" of your life, were there any red flags you ignored? When we are playing the greatness game, we use all the assets we have, and intuition is one of those assets. It will help keep you on track.

Social media likes, shares and comments don't measure your self-worth. It's not a replacement for the work you need to do to build your self-worth and self-esteem. They are called SELF-esteem and SELF-worth because they're an inside job through self-acceptance — just as you are and just as you aren't. Be real, be yourself and be authentic, and know that not everyone will like you, and that's OK.

When we try to prove ourselves to others to gain acceptance or validation, that is your smallness wanting to make you distrust yourself. #crushsmallness

The Greatness Money

Money is one of those things that you either love or hate talking about with others. I finally had enough in 2010. I had to stop the madness. I learned the skill sets to earn it, budget it, save it, invest it and spend it correctly. It was not a fun journey, but it was worth it! I was sick of being a slave to money and not seeing bigger returns. It's easy to become a victim of time and money, so these are a few of my favorite tips to win your Greatness Game in Money.

You might think that having a budget is limiting, but it's freeing. Living on a budget is all about telling your money "where to go" that way you are funding what is *important to you*. Winning your money game will make a huge difference for your present, future, vacations, investments, fun, dreams, giving and legacy. Whatever money game you want to win check out the books by Dave Ramsey they are the best on the planet.

Whatever greatness game you are playing, *play to win,* don't just play to play. When you play to play, you are working in vagueness, and you will often lack the intentionality to finish. When you play to win, there is a focus and clarity, and you finish and win. Greatness moves the train and wins the game. You are worth it.

Do you know what you want? Can you articulate the top three goals, dreams or desires that you want right now and how much you need to save to make them happen? Sometimes you bury your dreams because of a smallness belief, like "I can't afford it" or "I could never make that happen because it's too expensive." As long as you have that belief in place, you will be right. What would happen if you stopped agreeing with that thought? Would you rather be right or have your dream come true?

"Self-discipline begins with the mastery of your thoughts. If you don't control what you think about, you can't control what you do."

—NAPOLEON HILL

The trifecta of greatness: your voice, your money and your personal power are three big assets that you can use in significant ways. Are you using your trifecta to make a difference in the world or to run a business or to raise healthy children or start a movement? Be intentional *about how you are using these three elements,* and it will change the game.

If you are a business owner, you must keep your eyes on sales and marketing, or you will soon be building a hobby not a business. If you don't review your numbers each month and course correct depending on sales, chances are that you won't win. If sales and managing numbers are new skills (for most people they are), take classes on them. I was masterful in marketing but not in sales, and after taking some sales classes, I quadrupled my revenue. It's a skill set you can master, and it makes a huge difference.

The Greatness Parenting

Being a Mother is the biggest joy of my life. I'd never
experienced more love, joy and fun until I had my
daughter. She is the light of my life, and because I had
three failed pregnancies, I call her my miracle baby.
Every day, I want to be a better mom and navigate this
crazy journey with more grace. The hardest thing I
struggle with is getting dinner on the table every night,
but I'm always learning tips and resources to help. These
are a few of my favorite tips to win your Greatness Game
in Parenting.

You only have 18 summers with your kids until they go off into the world. Those 18 years are your time to be intentional. There's so much to teach them, but don't forget about these five: your family values and faith, self-management skills, choice-making skills, money management skills and self-esteem skills. See the book list in the back for my reading recommendation if you have kids in high school, heading to college.

Build a great family culture. It could be through bedtime routines, holiday traditions or simple family nights. Just imagine your child is in college explaining his or her "home life" to their friends and they use one word. What would *you want* that one word to be? Once you know what that one word is, you can start to create a culture and activities around it.

As a parent your outer voice becomes their inner voice, so when you are correcting, criticizing or condemning children, it can be the reason they start to live in their smallness. Choose your words wisely. If you need more parenting tips check out my parenting board on Pinterest.com/DenaPatton

Children go where there is excitement.
They stay where there is love.

- ZIG ZIGLAR

The longest relationship we will have is with ourselves, and our kids watch how we *treat and talk* about ourselves. Be kind and respect yourself because you are teaching your kids to do the same.

Whatever "hard phase" you or your kids are in right now, remember it will not last forever, but sometimes we forget that.

Know the difference between enabling and empowering your kids (or friends, employees, spouse). Be courageous to give them opportunities to take on responsibility without doing it for them.

We are "hungry" for our gifts and greatness to be in the world, but sometimes we get scared, and then we stuff those feelings with food (and other coping mechanisms). I've been there too, and I put a sign in the refrigerator for a year that said, "What you are hungry for is NOT in here." Eat when you are hungry, and not when you are scared. It takes courage to get your gifts and greatness in the world, and it's OK to be afraid. Do it anyway.

The Greatness Girls

Out of all the causes to stand for, I stand for girls. It moves my heart when a girl finds her voice, her greatness and her valuable place in the world. I honestly believe that girls change the world. I encourage you to hire more women and girls for your company and see the difference they make. Follow my girl's movement on Facebook @girlsrulefoundation or #girlschangetheworld. As Harvard University President Emeritus and former Chief Economist at the World Bank Lawrence Summers said, "Investment in girls' education may well be the highest-return investment available in the developing world."

You have the power over your gifts, your greatness, your dreams and your choices. But you don't have the power over other people's opinions or judgments. There will be haters, drainers and smallness people along your greatness journey who will hate, judge or give you an opinion. You have the power to believe them or not. Don't let their views turn into a label that you wear the rest of your life. Rip that label off.

In your teen years, focus on changing the world, not changing diapers. Children are a blessing, but wait until you are older and in marriage. Only 50 percent of teen mothers graduate from high school, and only 2 percent of teen mothers earn a college degree. Keep focusing on your big dreams because girls change the world.

No matter what your age; the world needs your dreams, your voice and your greatness. Don't let smallness tell you otherwise. #crushsmallness

Brynne Smith was a beautiful young lady who struggled with self-esteem as a girl, but then she found her voice, her power and her valuable place in the world. She became passionate to help other girls know their worth. Unfortunately, her life was cut short because of a helicopter accident, but today her legacy lives on because of her passion. She would encourage you to know your worth, and not be afraid to be the change you want to see in the world.

What do you want to solve in the world? If you could solve one problem and get paid well for it what would it be? Consider that solving the problem might be a career choice for you? Do some research on it to find out.

Each day is a new beginning. Today, start fresh in your greatness and go from there.

If you want straight As in school, then you need to BE an A student. Think like it, act like it, work like it. Reflect on how A students act. They sit in front, ask questions, pay attention, get in a study group, do their homework early, take pride in their work and ask for help when needed. You can't BE a D student and expect an A grade.

Girls, it is crucial that you learn from a young age to believe in yourself, but it's also important to understand how to take care of yourself. Your mind, body and spirit are precious, and it's your responsibility to take care of them.

Some people in this world are takers, drainers and haters. They can't affect you if you don't allow them. When you know your value, and you know your boundaries, they will not be able to use you or make you feel inferior. Give yourself permission to have clear boundaries with your money, work, energy, body and time.

"No one can make you feel inferior
without your consent"
– ELEANOR ROOSEVELT

Don't forget to celebrate all the progress, wins and achievements that you have accomplished. That's why it's important to have a winning wall. It reminds you of how far you have come when you have forgotten. Get your winning wall up today. #winningwall

You matter.

You are worthy.

You are brilliant, beautiful and bold just as you are.

Never let anyone tell you otherwise.

If you are a teen girl who loves to lead things and you have big dreams, look into a program called dreamLAB, which is a 12-week after-school club (www.dreamlabforgirls.org). It's where girls go to build their leadership, friendships and bright futures. I believe that girls with dreams become women with vision.

Never stop learning how to grow your self-management, self-discipline and self-esteem. Your future career, marriage, income and fulfillment will thank you for it.

When self-esteem is low, bad choices tend to be high. Self-esteem isn't just about "feeling good," it's the root of how you live, choose and act. When you have low self-esteem, you could be allowing people to treat you poorly or even abusively, or you could be treating others badly. The opposite of low self-esteem is egotistical/narcissistic, but the healthy middle is listening to your greatness in self-acceptance.

Living from your greatness isn't about proving you are enough because it knows you are enough. But society, advertising companies and smallness do not want you to know that. Greatness is the positive, loving and encouraging voice that we were all born with, and it knows that you are enough. You have the choice to believe your smallness or believe your greatness. Your life goes according to what you believe.

> "We are what we believe we are."
> —C.W. LEWIS

Love should never hurt, yet 33 percent of teen relationships are abusive or violent. It's important to learn what a healthy relationship looks like and what an unhealthy relationship looks like. People who use their power to control you have a tenacity also to be abusive. Choose wisely. Download the Red Flags Checklist and more tools at http://www.gopurple.org/for-teens.html.

When you are dreaming or planning your bright future, don't be vague. You want to move OUT of Vagueville! Clarity moves the train. Get clear in what you want and take action.

Keep dreaming from your greatness and don't quit on yourself. It took the current Miss Arizona six years of competitions to win the title and go on to Miss America. It took the Cubs 108 years to win the World Series. Michael Jordan has missed 9000 basketball shots and lost 300 games and was still one of the best basketball players. If you want to be inspired, read about successful people who didn't quit or who faced adversity and eventually fulfilled their dreams.

Questions For You

Take your thoughts to actions.

1. What are the greatness games that you are choosing to focus on for the next three months?

2. Where are you going to set up your #winningwall? (digitally? journal? office wall? bedroom wall?)

3. Are you accepting the #crushsmallness challenge for the next 30 days? This is where you turn down your smallness every time you hear it. What is the main "smallness statement" that deflates/ disempowers you when you hear it?

4. This is about thinking differently. This is about mastering a #greatnessonly mindset, and doing this challenge with someone is optimal. Who are you going to ask to be your buddy/pair/greatness partner to accomplish the 30 day challenge with? (Support each other and every time you turn down smallness you text them #crushsmallness)

5. Have you downloaded Dena's Greatness Daily Mantra to help you get centered in your greatness every morning?
    (located at www.amazinggreatness.com)

    Yes   No   I'm going to create my own

Books I referred to and recommend

MARRIAGE:

- "The 5 Love Languages" by Gary Chapman
- "Love & Respect" by Dr. Emerson Eggerichs

LIFE:

- "Aspire" by Kevin Hall
- "The Invitation" by Oriah Mountain Dreamer

LEADERSHIP:

- "10-10-10: A Life-Transforming Idea" by Suzy Welch
- "Values, Inc." by Dina Dwyer-Owens
- "Tribes" by Seth Godin
- "No Excuses: Nine Ways Women Can Change How We Think About Power" by Gloria Feldt

FAITH:

- "Lioness Arising" by Lisa Bevere
- "The Purpose Driven Life" by Rick Warren
- "Closed Sundays" by Nicole Gebhardt

MONEY:

- "Financial Peace University" by Dave Ramsey (book or class)

GIRLS:

- "My Feet Aren't Ugly: A girl's guide to loving herself from the inside out" by Debra Beck
- "1001 Things Every College Student Needs to Know" by Harry H Harrison Jr

Work with Dena

How can you develop or sustain your greatness games in bigger ways?

Everything Dena creates is to help you win your greatness games, and she has six main ways to serve you:

1. Join her Greatness Community for ongoing support and coaching at: www.thegreatnessgamecommunity.com

2. Hire her to speak at your business conference, women's retreat or event.

3. Attend one of her Jump Into Greatness: Skydiving Mastermind days in Phoenix.

4. Work with her as a coach in a VIP day or get private coaching.

5. Read her Igniting Greatness Blog free on her website.

6. Hire Dena to bring her Greatness Team Training to your corporation or team.

Read more details at: www.DenaPatton.com

About Dena Patton

Dena sold her marketing and PR company in NYC in 1999 to follow her dreams to share greatness in the world. She became a global speaker, best selling author and business coach who works with leaders, entrepreneurs and world changers. She has been an award-winning entrepreneur since 1996 and a full-time coach since 2001, helping clients create GREAT businesses and become GREAT leaders. She is the creator of Greatness Coaching and The Greatness Marketing Academy, and she believes in creating well-oiled, well-marketed and well-led businesses that *do well* so they can *do good*. She loves speaking, hosting skydiving masterminds, and leading three-day retreats to help others win their greatness games. Besides igniting greatness in the world, she is also passionate about the empowerment and leadership of women and girls as the co-founder of www.GirlsRuleFoundation.org, a 501c3 where $1 of each of these books will be donated. She lives in Phoenix, Ariz., with her husband, Greg, and their daughter, Alexandra, who is an artist and contributed her illustration to this book. Read more about her: www.DenaPatton.com

Connect with Dena:

FACEBOOK: @DenaPatton
INSTAGRAM: @DenaMariePatton
PINTEREST: @DenaPatton

GREATNESS BLOG: www.DenaPatton.com

FOR DENA'S DAILY GREATNESS MANTRA AND
OTHER FREE DOWNLOADS: www.amazinggreatness.com

CPSIA information can be obtained
at www.ICGtesting.com
Printed in the USA
FSHW04n0926210318
45772FS